Too Heavy to Carry

Too Heavy to Carry

Cat Dixon

Stephen F. Austin State University Press
Nacogdoches, Texas

For information address:
Stephen F. Austin State University Press
1936 North Street, LAN 203
Nacogdoches, TX 75962

sfapress@sfasu.edu

Book Design: Laura Davis, Troy Varvel
Cover Design: Troy Varvel
Cover Art: Erin Michelle Bonen
Author Photo: g thompson higgins photography

LIBRARY OF CONGRESS CATALOGING-IN-PUBLICATION DATA

Dixon, Cat
Too Heavy To Carry/Cat Dixon—1st ed.
p.cm
ISBN 978-1-62288-056-0

I. Title

First Edition: 2014

"Some people have to try just a little bit harder
Before their life's work is done."

--Brenda Lee, from the song "Too Heavy to Carry"

CONTENTS

TOO HEAVY TO CARRY

THE BEARDED HOMELESS MAN COMES TO THE UNITARIAN CHURCH DOOR

I bring him a jar of peanut butter
and a loaf of bread.

>*"You got anything else?"*

He won't take this offering.

Rummaging through the kitchen, I find
a box of breakfast bars—never opened—
I bring them to the door.

>He frowns. He doesn't like these either.

I take him the left-over Easter candy.
Bags of it had been sitting on the counter for weeks.

>*"Oh! Candy! Yes!"*

Like a man panning for hours, finally securing
one nugget, he is overjoyed with
the blueflowered bucket
and bags of M&M's and Reese's Pieces.

He marches off with his treasure
again the little boy he once was—
Easter morning finally here—candy-filled eggs,
the basket of goodies beside his bedroom door.

Three weeks later, he's back.
Cheryll answers the door.
He tells her he has lost 25 family members
in the last year—this time
an elaborate story. She gives him
a gift card to Burger King. He leaves.
He doesn't really want to discuss
the people, the things he's lost.

Cheryll says she gets him—
if she were homeless, she'd want
candy, booze, smokes and drugs.

He comes again in the autumn with a new coat,
new camouflage pants.

MATTHEW 13:33

I give you and you and you
a ball of dough, then, later,
days later, ask a few
to my kitchen. I have three
rolling pins for five women.
I knead the bread like I would
massage my husband's wide back
yet this mass is smooth and spotless.
While waiting for the rise,
we reluctantly chitchat,
lop off words before
we can finish, gnawing at our nails,
savage from the smell.

COMMISERATING WITH ANOTHER PARENT

You tell me you feel the same—
procreation was a mistake—
all of this while sharing bottles
of hotel wine on a patio. I'd buy
the whole bar just to sit under
these country stars and have
an ally. No one has ever
agreed with me before and as you
pour, we talk of childless times—
before—all grand.
We pretend it's that time again.
The mosquitoes buzz into
the sweet bottles. We watch
as they fly inside the glass—
then you cork them, trapped.

Daughters Over Sons

I.

Leven, your teeth are so white, straight and perfect like little sugar cubes. I want to pluck them out of the pink cake of your gums and suck on them for hours until there's a gritty residue along my lips. In fourth grade my friend and I made a house out of sugar cubes. We used glue as our mortar, but we kept eating the bricks. Finally we resolved to eat no more, so we dabbed glue on every piece to save them. Your mouth, from where screams and giggles escape, is that candy house with your tongue a carpet of cherry taffy and all want to partake.

II.

Leven, when I was a girl things were pink—embarrassing pink—pink pig book bag, large hot pink winter coat, Barbie's dresses, Barbie's corvette, then, McDonald's, soap operas, trailers, scratching my face at night until it bled, missing my father. I want you to know me, know your father, know that once I snuggled him at night and prayed for him to be safe when he raced off to fire calls. I danced with him in the room that is now yours to Bruce all night and kissed him, and I will never love like that again nor should I. Life came from that. "No more babies," I declared when I arrived to have my tubes burnt away like a controlled forest fire, but nothing is controlled. Everything is scorched. Even my tongue has blisters. Electric currents run from my fingertips when we pass you back and forth and I watch how he plays with you—lifting you by the arms which I want to say is dangerous, but I don't because you giggle a little girl giggle and the only memory I have of my father like that is when I was five or six and he took my foot into his mouth, wet and warm, told me he was going to eat it—my leg extended into the air like a kick and I'm sure I laughed like you, but I don't remember.

III.

Leven, I was stuffing my face with everything in the world trying to devour the scent of you and cookies and trees and locker rooms. Attempts all futile, but I didn't care. Losing air and my balance, I fell to the ground with a thud. I remember your first steps in a circle holding a battery-operated play drum that I have recently given away. I couldn't listen to its songs anymore—reminded me of when you were a thunderous ballerina with no patience and when you started to move, you wouldn't stop and it was so soon—too soon. Now I am alone. Here, waiting for you to return to the baby I wanted, needed, and knowing that will never happen, you say *goo goo* as a joke now and you pooped in the potty like a big girl and I'm left broken on the floor, the size of an elephant. If you can't get them to come back, feed the dreams fast food and blues and grape vodka and hope beyond hope that somehow time will reverse. That little 11-month-old prancer will wander back and I will not be here, eating and eating, my throat about to explode, the whole load of the universe comprised of donut holes and Tootsie rolls. You're made of pinwheels and curls and the damp, musty smell of a once-flooded basement. The sky cries for a month knowing you will love me—you will never know me.

IV.

Leven, from heaven, favorite number is seven or eleven, will marry a guy named Kevin and will only eat unleavened bread. Oh Leven, you can tell your mother has lost her mind when she rhymes your name and then cuts it apart to *Eve*—the first woman and then *Lev*—the nickname of a rockstar's skinny daughter I am sure, and then *Even*. You *will* get even someday.

Steppe

There, sir. You're trapped
on my leeward side
in rain shadow, yet,
won't ask for water, help
or touch. The cactus cage
pricks palms into voodoo dolls.
The humidity suffocates
like a young, naïve wife.

Come now, bandage up.
The injuries to your hands
fester, a microcosm of us,
a tiny volcano of pus.

OUTCROP

He asks me to study him in situ. He says I'll know all I'll need to know, then. I go. He is a porcupine that shoots needles at me every time I mention love or distance. I scurry persistently around the bedrock, measuring the exposed chips, lines to determine how one could evolve from this to that. Fossils tie my ponytail back, make creases in my hands more apparent every time I wash dishes or babies' bottles. He never grows old and his allegories never make much sense. How can a porcupine kiss and dance? How can he, small, spiny, and smart, calculate the odds and not take the chance? After dimensions are retrieved, I leave—head home to examine the evidence, the graphs to record my final analysis.

THE WINTER MOTH ORBITS THE LIGHT

and her axis is not slowed
by flaps of wings. though her
movements erratic, the effect
is to eradicate the night,
to prevent confusion, cold.
for this, she has flung
all hope into the static
pulse of wings. she's a kite
controlled by gusts, not to fold
or bend despite the sling
shot maneuvering her frantic
flight plan has mapped. she fights,
it seems, to snap the bow
and arrow, to burn her wings
on the sun, to reach manic.

WITH THE ZOOLOGIST IN THE CLOSED EXHIBIT

When he grabs the snake, its mouth opens in slow motion,
as if it will swallow him, me, the habitat; I see each tooth,
and in each tooth is a baby mouse. With the other
gloved hand, he plucks at a mouse, the pink tail the umbilical cord,
and he must tug, jerking it loose, and another mouse appears. I never knew
snake teeth bred mice. The baby mice soon carpet the dirt
and he extracts them while I cower by the entry,
my hands over my mouth as if my teeth, too, will give birth.

CIRCUS MAN

He juggled—
not the way a child might toss three balls
and keep them in the air like popcorn, no,
he juggled fire without scorching his skin.
He tossed blocks, batons, bowling pins, and apples
and he could keep them in the air
for ten minutes straight—his eyes bouncing
as well and I just watched.

He balanced
on that trapeze for years with no net to catch him.

He unicycled blindfolded past the crowd
and survived the obstacle course—pleas, cries, suicide attempts.

He scooped the elephant shit,
the peanut shells, the popcorn kernels.

He tamed every lion, but his own.

BLACK CAT

I didn't cut my arms or hide
the marks beneath long sleeves.
It was the cat. The scars,
an unreadable alphabet
on my skin, tell stories of how
evil cats really are. Somehow
the cat had also cut a chunk
out of my thumb; it's a silver moon,
a backwards C that marks her territory.

I clung to that shiny moon—
a groping trapeze artist
and every full moon sky
spotlighted my maneuverings,
my pent-up rage at the stars,
the craters, the endless black cat
who whips her tail this way
and that, who grows fat on meteors
and blackholes, who purrs and her
purring fills my mouth with fur.

TANSTAAFL

when my tail whips the corner, jetting to the litter box or the food, don't blame me.   i warned you. dab your eyes, fluff your hair, mimic the saunter of the feline as you wait for me to return. turn your nose up at all invitations. i've been intimate with every corner of this house: the comforter, the toilet bowl, the fish bowl. the owner calls me obsolete. i am threatened with the dumpster, the shelter. don't lower your eyes. don't settle for white lies. ten years ago on the patio I stooped to help something nameless—was it a rodent? was it a child? and that has made all the difference.

BEARDED SWIMMER

> *Helge Meeuw at the 2008 German Swimming Championships in*
> *Berlin made a new European record in the 100 meter backstroke. At*
> *the men's relay in the 2008 Olympics in Beijing, he placed last in a*
> *race. The commentators said of his bearded face:*
>> Commentator 1: *Why wouldn't he shave that?*
>> Commentator 2: *Why risk it?*
>> Commentator 1: *That's crazy.*

Maybe he wanted to be different:
all the competitors, hairless fish,
tiny goggles suctioned to their faces,
flattened, indented chests,
long bodies, speedy eels,
all identical to trout fighting upstream
to the undeniable.

Maybe his sweetheart, Helene, told
him the beard improved
his strength, a Samsonite athlete.
Suddenly his razor and shaving
gel vanished. She swore on
her father's grave she hadn't
done it; convinced him
of her reasoning.

Or he had been swallowed by that
great, gray whale. Inside the hollow
mouth, he swam from its teeth
to its tongue, back and forth
for years, a bowled goldfish,
and he now knew
escape was unattainable.

At the Catfish Symposium

Released from the reservoir,
fish swim directionless. How often
had they dreamed of this day
when the water would flow;
the walls, a giant playpen,
folded, carried away;
when they may mingle—
their mouths open, no longer
waiting for pacifiers, but hooks. The lines
delivering from disease.

THE REEF

The calcium exoskeleton is
broken and made holy
by the waves, by the encasement

of each new polyp. The coral head grows
as it, too, is fragmented into tiny
rooms for every fish,

crab and sponge. Every night
the darkness and seaweed hide
Parrotfish as he slowly wades

to Angelfish's apartment. Her place
past the balconies, past the dark violet
urchins, is crowded and algae-

filled. Parrotfish has
a booming voice once inside. Angelfish
whines and many times

snappers have been sent to resolve
loud disputes erupting from Angel's
residence, yet, the lovers have always

found their way to reconcile even
when her mother scolded her
or Parrot was dragged out

by the reef's edge and given
"the talk." Later, he'd sweetly tell
Angel how her eyes were as beautiful

as the walls' twinned hexagonal crystals.
Angel would say he moved
as gracefully as Jellyfish and all night

they whispered similes, swaying
dreamingly with the water,
as if only they lived in this place.

WATER

I just want water.
My friend says to drink Smart Water.

What makes it "smart"?

Is it that it's bottled and expensive,
and it's in pretty plastic?

Is it that most folks cannot afford it?

Is it that the water has a name: "Glaceau"
that sounds like the word glacier,
or is it that the company has added
electrolytes for taste as if the water
the earth provided didn't taste good enough?

But we've destroyed all that water,
haven't we? Almost all.

And the last bit left—
the aquifer—we want to drench, to douse
with oil from a TransCanada Pipeline.

Oh yes, dear ones, this water
is so "smart" after all.

BUTTE

My prolonged loneliness doesn't compute.
Once, I was much desired for I was cute.

Now, I'm more of an old coot
wandering here to there hooting

and carrying on as if I could shoot
a man with an arrow; emotion take root

in this shallow soil. All the fruit
has decayed and I must follow suit.

The sharp land has been looted
by rains and unquestionable absolutes.

I'll never be her again, astute,
thin. I throw down the flute. Go mute.

HOODOOS

I.

The landscape is comprised of dead bodies: thousands of giants were murdered not by vengeful gods, no, instead, they were exterminated along with the dinosaurs when that fateful asteroid plummeted to our planet sending ash heavenward, then it rained black tears, raven's feathers, as if the world could cry forever and the bodies of every giant from the Aloads to Dante's Nimrod, the babbling fool, who had not even been written of, fell, buried beneath the dirt. With their last gasp, each raised his hand, a gallant effort clinging to the blue now hidden by gray clouds. Now, in the badlands, one can see their arms extended, their color darker at the elbows, their fingernails strengthen the tops compared to the soft rock of their arms' flesh. Underground, they kick their legs, not encased in rock, causing earthquakes, volcanoes and all unrest.

II.

Commander and Chief, Satan, has lined his rockets up in uneven rows, some Parisian cemetery where organization doesn't matter, and a confused state makes it all the better, aiming them toward heaven. The silent missiles wait for the button to be pushed, for the alarm to sound like private school children kneeling at Mass daydreaming about sex while the priest turns the wafer into flesh, listening for the *Amen* to signal the time to stand and sing. When will the day come? Satan claims to know, but his angels doubt his stratagems or intelligence. They have no spies in heaven, no way to know for sure when God and Jesus will finally be asleep for the launch to be worthwhile, so for now, they wait.

A Wild Boar Stampedes My House at Night

In bed, I'm awakened by the snarls of a boar revving like my overweight husband's snores, but no, the ugly brown animal and its sharp tusks stand at the bedroom door. Sent by my husband's whore, it chases me. My husband is gone. Down the hall my naked three-year-old's legs pump, his little bottom tenses. Around the kitchen island he goes, the boar at his heels. The pots and pans crash from above: metallic wind chimes. I jump onto the glass-top dining room table, usually unstable, but now holds my weight. I bend down, snatch my son's arm, pluck him effortlessly like a flower from the ground. Then hold him, legs wrapped tightly around my waist. The beast huffs and puffs, and I want to tell my son how this is the big bad wolf—our dining room table, the brick house, and we are the smart little pig, but that's just a story we tell. The circle of glass begins to wobble when the boar rams its head beneath us. My friend Shawna enters the front door, shouts, and the boar turns interested in the large, six-foot tall woman. It pounds down the stairs to attack her. Prepared for battle, she choke-holds the boar as soon as it reaches the foyer. I scream, *"Kill it! Kill it!"* like I did to my husband when I came upon a spider. He'd pick up a shoe and smash the spider flat, but he never moved fast enough. Did it matter which shoe he used? Must he walk so slowly? Did he not know a spider in *my* house was an emergency? Shawna and the boar wrestle. She on top, then the animal. All I see is her hair, its fur. Again at Shawna, I shout, *"Kill it! Kill it!"* Impatient, shaking, I lower my son and myself off the table to view the fight better. They struggle as if under water, desperately seeking the surface, but holding each back from oxygen. The boar breaks free. Shawna lunges, misses. The tusks come, sharp, upturned. I guard my son, but the boar sent here for a duty, charges past me on the right to my child, lowers its head, then pierces the toddler's testicles with the left horn. Like a pale flag, the boar carries my son high in the air above its head. I kick and screech at the animal, but it doesn't attack me. From behind, Shawna shoots the boar with a .22, and it falls dead—one bullet to the head. Then she kneels, gently slides the dirty tusk from my son's delicate pink skin like she takes an earring off at the end of a date night with her spouse. *"If you had that, why didn't you use it before, you idiot!"* I roar. I recall the evenings after we put our son to bed how I'd rant at my husband over our sexless existence, over how he could use Viagra with his mistress, but not with me. I pick the child up, hold him in my arms, and apologize for the boar. I leave Shawna to clean up the mess.

BIRD BY BIRD—SHE SAYS SHE IS A WRITER!

Car by car he drove past
to his nooner. He imagined

them together
for life—her husband dead;

me, by and by, away—
divorced. Suit by suit clinked

on the dry cleaner's rack, a diary's
pages, I'd never see.

I washed undershirts
and underwear. Slip

by slip piled on his desk,
a hill of debt, shuffled

under a report or a coworker's
note; he paid for every motel

trip. Playing with our son after
work, he'd stop every few minutes

to check, check, check his BlackBerry;
a man hooked, gutted by meaningless

beckoning. Tree by tree I lead
the woman to a place for hanging

by her ratty, gold hair.
Bird by bird chirped along my street.

GULLY

By a farm on a hill was a tree. Me.
For decades I was peacefully
standing, a hostess seating
birds, squirrels, leaves and even
a beehive for a time, and I saw
the small erosion, thought nothing
of it till the land, like a throat
was opened and roots, bloody
tendons, shot forth.
Then it was all downhill
from there. I began to rot
and the other trees
slowly slipped onto a conveyor
belt of mud and sludge
with a rodent sliding us
over a scanner:
beep, beep, beep.

TO THE FATHER OF MY CHILDREN

"In a certain state it is indecent to go on living."

—Friedrich Nietzsche

I do not grow. I could
plant myself here
or there, wherever—see,
soil spits me out—
a bloated seed never
to green. I change
pots, yards, repeatedly,
yet, I yield nothing.
I would've uprooted myself last
time had I not
been directionless. Found along
the highway, buttes
and to those a thought took
root, but it was exceedingly clear
the southern winds meant
to tangle slips of paper
into tumbleweed notebooks;
to throw dust into eyes
and mouths—bury the corpses
who still walk, want to talk. The trees
dance in place as if it were
exercise, and their lust for
movement turns the land
into that circle of hell. I reenter,
my hollow city,
whose name begins with the letter
"O." How can one go home
to an empty hole? If
I trace the circle I'd erode
a pit, a grave for the full moon
to rest; extricate the ground
water to clean the craters
(a cosmic undertaker), all to

demonstrate I'm Pilate---I must
wash myself of this. Excused,
unsuitable for any terrain,
unsettled by gusts, the constant
displacement, waiting, a giant
beak cracks me in half
and then, Mark, you'll have the last laugh.

Best,
Catharine

ONCE A WOMAN

At my summit there is no
view, no cloud, no bird.
Only a dancing, dark-haired clown,
who squawks with arms flapping
as if to flag down a rescue plane,
but no one flies this way.

A man places a piece of me
on his desk, a memento
from a rock-climbing expedition.
          "Here," he brags to coworkers.
          "I survived Catharine."

He returns to his cubicle walls
still covered with pictures
of our children. He takes
down the photo of me:
22, unblemished skin, brown curly hair
and tosses it.

After office hours,
a janitor retrieves the picture
from the trash can.
She touches the rock
on the desk and imagines
the time it took to create
such a thing. Now sitting in his chair,
examining the photos not discarded,
she thinks of her daughters, her infant grandson,
the mountains of trash she's had
to collect in office after office
to support the kids. The earth
presses into itself
to make a glittering rock.

FORMATION

you are building a tower on an island in the middle
of the sea; resurrecting sleep; learning to sleep

alone. sleep like gravity pulls down on your head,
your pile of bedding. in the early oceans, poseidon
created each stone, each formation, then flung

them from his bed. there, geologists study how a beautiful facies
came to be. layer after layer shiny on your queen-size
island; layer after layer, free.

BLACK STING RAY

God will forgive each
baptism. My red hair doused in
gasoline as I jeep along climbing hills
like a sunrise. Let's rise to the moon, then Mars
before reaching Paris in spring in bloom:
pink, red, green, deep saucy blue. Much easier
this way. I didn't have the rope
to hang from the balcony back there;
in bloody bathwater I kept floating,
slipping from plankton
piece to plankton piece.

Here, drink in daydreams
like nail polish remover to burn
away taste buds and tonsils.
Walk the downtown streets
in Chicago. A hotel match is lit
by a shaky smoker and thrown next
to my heart visiting your feet for the day.

ADRENAL OVER HEART

mismatched, resting on bags, bitty diamonds invisible to the mouth.

the phone rings. he lets it go to voicemail. it's probably silence. it's always silence.

on the 15th of april on a baseball diamond i met kerri who knew kelly.

this time the receiver picked up the signal.

my muscle continues to palpitate, to race, to mutate as it aches with caffeine.

dial the number. 4-3-5. snap the phone shut. he will never call again.

fight or flight. flight or fight. freeze or flight. flight or freeze. freeze or fight. fight or freeze. fuck or freeze. freeze or fuck.

hundreds of prairie dogs dash notes from hole to hole as if they're the signals from some universal radio; distressed, he relates stories of shrews.

the cap breaks and my blood spatters the nurse's blue gloved hands.

the prairie dogs race faster. on the edge of the field, our legs nipped by mosquitoes, the concession stand closed, he remarks on the loss of pay phones—another extinction.

RIVER

Weeks ago when the city's sewage operators dumped shit into the Missouri, people were warned not to swim, boat or fish in the water, yet, there was a white boat out there, always one guy who didn't see the newscast or who just didn't give a fuck, on his 30-foot cruiser, blared music, wasting his batteries and letting his five-year-old aboard without a life jacket. That time. Weeks ago when the river was just a giant's toilet, a corroded pipe to the ocean, I needed to sit on the bank then. I did. My gray SUV's back hatch open wide like a yawn, my legs hanging from the bumper. There I sat. I drank Smirnoff straight. It tasted gray. I drank amaretto —my baby's breath after she suckled. The wind blew; water rippled the stars. Drunk and nauseous from the smell, the chiggers bit me, the fireflies were candles to light my way, the mosquitoes drew my blood, took samples of it to some insect lab where every test came back positive, I strolled by the river's edge. I can't swim. Wading in, my brown flip-flops slipped off, my shirt and jeans weighed me down, my rocks. I can't back-float. I almost drowned in eighth grade. How disappointed I was with my savior, a bigger girl named Kay, who scooped me up as if I were a penny in a fountain. She had retrieved my wish so she could throw in her own, but that was Beaver Lake, this is the Missouri. I'll trudge forward into the current. The toilet will flush. My vomit, the night before, was silt-colored and I stared at it for hours. There, in my bathroom, I saw the bottom of the river. Everything that is too heavy to carry on, rests.

"THE CHILD I NEVER HAD."
 – Jorge Luis Borges

You, my child, have given me shoulders as heavy as Atlas' and have corked my mouth so I can't articulate what I really mean. You, a catch-22, stole my amaretto and made sure that a divorce will never be final and yet, I can't leave you be—to maim your helmetless head biking in the street or to strangle yourself with the cord hanging from the blinds or to wander off to live in the woods with the animals or to run with a butcher knife and to see with one less eye. I can't regret your nonexistence and I will not regret your birth. When I look at you now, you, unknowing that I would've ended you before you even took a breath until I read Borges' words; you, a little boy with dark eyes like my mother's; you, whose whine is an alarm that I must shut off immediately; you, who dance ballet and have arms that twirl like helicopter blades, you are mine.

SUNDAY AFTERNOON AT MISSION PARK

My son and I survey the trees,
novice birdwatchers, to listen for chirps.
Instead of climbing on the play equipment
or sliding down the blue slide,
Pierce collects sticks that litter
the woodchips from last week's
storm. He, the preschool-sized
groundskeeper, hauls the pile
to the trash can and heads
to retrieve more debris.
Overhead the serenade starts again:
Pierce, Pierce, Pierce, Pierce, Pierce.

To find the bird, to know its name,
I want to climb the tree, to ascend
to the highest branch so I can write
about this bird that whistles
my son's name so clearly, and Pierce,
his arms akimbo, his brow scrunched,
smirks and asks,
"Why that bird say my name?"
It calls over and over, a joyful peck,
a canticle to a tiny god.

Bathroom Photo

My three-year-old son sits naked on the potty,
just out of a bath. I drape a gray towel over him.
Now covered, he's a shivering
monster perched on porcelain.
I ask if he's done. He won't respond,
so I grab my camera; snap a photo
to share with his fiancé when he brings
her home during winter break and when
I've nothing to say, I'll take her to the frame,
hidden behind another; let her hold it
and tell her how once Pierce
almost pooped in the tub when he was three,
how I bathed him and he was small
enough for me to carry wrapped up
in a towel to his room
to rub lotion all over his skin.

FARM

When Mother was sick, Daughter ran
the place though she was the youngest.
In every litter there's a runt.
It can't fight to suckle. Its squeals
drive the sow to squash, then
suffocate the blind piglet.

By the pigpen, Daughter would
stay for hours when the sow
gave birth. Which one didn't belong?
She read the clouds, the birds,
she knew: a storm's coming,
loud, thunderous.

She'd watch the piglet shrivel
in just one day, one hour
to a sun-dried, red raisin.
Still it cried. Waiting.
It seemed the right thing to do.
Pluck the piglet from the rest,
hold it by the wiry tail, then slam
the body against the brick wall.

Again. The eyes pop forth,
wild ricocheting bingo balls set
free from their cage; the blood
smacked and sprayed, an attempt
at Pollock with a bloated
paintbrush. Toss the body away.
See relief in the sow's eyes.

Years later, when Daughter learned she was
having a girl, she decorated
the nursery: walls, delicate green;
furniture, white as paper;
curtains, lacy pink, a crochet

of piglet tails; the rug hand-woven;
baskets to hold everything.
She waited with the patience
learned from the barn. Seasons
came to birth bright crops,
to harvest death: a cycle:
rain and sun, drought
and flood. During the birth,
she lost so much blood, the doctor
almost called it, but tornadoes
twist away.

Night after night her feet padded
through the nursery door. The baby
wouldn't hush, latch or sleep.
Her lips and skin so red
from crying, the piglet was
in her arms, a tiny oracle forecasting
a bad crop, a wolf on the loose,
a noose. It seemed the right thing to do.

ON HER SECOND BIRTHDAY

I'm eating, eating, eating her hair—
stringy, fine baby hair and I'm waiting,
waiting for the reverse of birth—
take her in again, quiet the tantrums.
Can the earth implode? Can volcanoes
suction up their magma once it has
become lava? Will the melted path
awaken—trees erect, skin return
to bone? When I laugh, she scratches
the back of my throat. When I rest,
I hear her groans.

After He Leaves the Barn

Every time I lie down
it's in that barn—
horses stomp their droppings
into brown lily pads;
a flick of a tail to shoo flies,
my only flag of surrender;
birds fly back and forth
in the rafters, free to go where
they chose. I've been loose
as those sparrows,
able to roam, to come and go,
but I always return
to the barn, nibbling
my fingernails till I taste blood.

WITH NO FATHER

I shrunk
to the size of an unlucky penny.

When I was sixteen,
Mom was too busy

with her young, blond boyfriend.
I learned from my friend, Maria,

how to do laundry;
whites and darks are separate.

Maria taught me scrambled eggs
and grilled cheese.

Her grandma would invite me to dinner
almost every week. Otherwise,

I ate alone.
Mom visited me monthly

with a few bags of groceries
and twenty dollar bills left

on the coffee table,
then she'd disappear again.

Sometimes I'd go see her
at the grocery store where

she worked. She wouldn't respond
to Mother, so I called, Juanita,

and her head would turn
like a cash register's drawer flying open

at the touch of the orange button.
My classmates who worked there

said that she must be a great mom.
I'd shrug.

She thought she could leave me
like one does money in an account,

where I'd grow, mature
and incur interest, ready to be

cashed out whenever
she felt like it.

He thought he could
deposit a monthly check

and be done with it.

WHIP HER WITH HAIR

When you strip her, bend her,
comb her, a crease forms

down the middle, between
her lungs—thinner than a cigarette.

She blows smoke out
the window as if it won't
circulate back inside—
as if she can hide
the burning flame—
heightened by breath.

She undulates like a ripped banner,
whipping the wind. She sends sheets
of paper out to sea like pigeons.

CHANCE

The hands shuffled the cards,
cracked them together like dozens
of knuckles. Then, the deal.
Cards, whirly-twirly
as Maple tree helicopter seeds,
whipped across the table.
Dizzy, they rested.

All facedown trimmed in blue
swirls, veins—lying
in wait—a tarot card reader
offered to line up her cards
like doors. She opened
their faces, pushed them closer.
They skated across the table
as if it were an ice rink. They stood
there shivering at my wrist.
I walked away.

When I met you, I didn't
know your story. I saw
only giant calves and running
shoes. I wanted to turn you
over. Flip! See your suite,
find your edges, keep you
out of the deck.

In Vegas, the Blackjack
table tempts me.
What luck! I've been
dealt an ace—it can go
either way. Do I hit or stand?
Never mind.
You play poker.

ATTACHMENT

If one catches a splinter
while hammering a canvas
into a frame, he should not
dig with tweezers at the fleck
thus tearing at his flesh
like a melodramatic griever.
Instead, he should
let it be stuck under
the skin, a reminder
of the chore, of the woman
in the painting.
The epidermis has a mind—
knows when it's hurt,
when it's cold, alone.
It will rid itself of what
it needs to soon
enough. The sliver
will free itself
without notice until
he sits down to write
a letter, takes up a pen,
and sees it's finally gone.

Placement

If one has all
the pieces to a puzzle,
one need not stay
awake through the night
to complete the picture, to hunt
down the missing piece
for one cannot know
which piece is missing
until one has
finished what there is.

When all pieces fall
together, let them sit
on a coffee table, gather
dust. Glue the puzzle
to a poster board, hang
it above the sofa and call it
good, then haggle over the best
spot on the wall.

FOR MY PAPA, ALFONSO ALBERTO LOPEZ DE NADA (ABEL) FROM TABASCO, ZACATECAS

Weighted down by eight or nine trunks,
the elephant tree, sluggish and bent
in need of more than one leg,
swayed, and it was here
that Abel rested in its shade;
decided to leave
his hometown, his sisters.
He never talked of the trees,
the land, the tinkering in shops
to earn flour and corn. Perhaps
Chicago with its taller buildings,
pool halls, beef sandwiches,
Italian women from Michigan helped.
But how could he forget?
The cactus would bristle at night
when the wind plowed the land,
when the stray dogs dug
up the bones of the dead. He'd
holler at them, but they'd
return again. They resorted to
cremation. Jesus would resurrect
without bone or flesh—
just ashes and white flecks.
Abel couldn't forget. Maybe
that's why he drank
his beer and whiskey.
When he didn't have cash, he drank
his wife's perfume and was found
in the bathroom one night sniffing
the rubbing alcohol. So, she had to hide
anything, anything, then have
him admitted to the hospital—
missed his only child's high school graduation,
the first in his family. Abel never
taught her Spanish—snapped at her

when she tried to mimic him
and his friends. He died when
she was 28. He never saw
her broken hearts or his only grandchild.

Abel, when that elephant tree stretches
out to the stars, that same tree, (let's
imagine it still stands there), do you
reach down from the sky to grasp
its trunk, to slide back to Zacatecas
to cross the river to visit me?

THE FALL OF ONE UNITARIAN CHURCH

The young office administrator,
young compared to most of the congregation,
waited with the patience of Joseph in the prison—
convicted of a crime she did not commit.
Lonely and forsaken, she built up
the crumbling walls like Nehemiah ,
and, yet, no one wrote down her prayers,
and she did not save a soul.

The minister emeritus with his smoky eyeglasses
and clouds of smoke trailing behind him in the sanctuary and up the stairwells,
waited with the patience and silence of a god
witnessing the golden calf's creation,
the molding and sculpting, then the worshipping,
then the sacrificing. The elderly minister took the pulpit
and read poetry. Even Robert Frost with his wisdom,
booming in the sanctuary's new speakers with the minister's
throaty, weighted voice, could not wake them.

Finally, all left. And still the two, the youngest and the oldest,
relax in the pew, fold the Sunday bulletins, push the keys on the
forbidden and cursed organ, still the two, recite poems for the rest of their days.

Tabula Rasa

From behind one-way glass,
I stare. The line-up
comprises him and him
and several more.
I point to each and each
is called forth—
come straight, turn to the side,
move to the back wall.

When asked who did it,
I say everyone.

The men sent to cells, the officers
go home, a janitor
sweeps by with a broom,
so I tap the glass,
call over the mike
to the narrow, empty tomb.

EULOGY FOR JOHN BERRYMAN

I sit down with a poet's book
—your book—to grieve the loss
like I knew you. You died
a decade before I came to life. O, I, too,
sprang from a cigarette ash flick,
an extra shot of tequila. I, too,
experienced the father's disappearing act, yet
I received cards and letters on holidays. Here,
at my cluttered desk, I imagine us
as friends, or lovers, or mentor and mentee.
No one writes like you. No one
sounds like you. Was it the boredom
that finally did you in, or was it
the incessant pounding on the eyelids—images,
phrases, that constipated everyday speech, that
gnawing: this is all bullshit? If I had
been there, I would've grabbed your hand and
begged you to take me with you. It seems
we are the only two who know that
everything is dust.

GLACIER

For Trent W.

Why live here instead of there? Does it matter?

> You live at the foot, the ice
> melts faster than it grows,
> and if you tilled the sheets
> you'd discover a rock,
> gravel, sawdust-like mound
> for the ice settles, thrusts, twists,
> a lover in a king-sized bed
> who can't sleep alone. I live
> where the ice thins
> to nothing. Everything is
> tinted blue like water. A duvet—
> sky, ice, ocean—blankets all.

Why assimilate the years I slept with another—
you alone, an iceberg calved below sea level
to jet towards the sky like a leaping fish—
unless we need to?

> Between us the brittle crevasses
> are God's dentures. He's taken
> them out for the night; left them
> in a bathroom tumbler
> soaking in Polident.
> He has a million mouths, teeth
> the size of doors and beds.
> A hundred chasms widen, the parts
> rub and touch deep below,
> but from above one cannot tell
> they even intersect.

Does God play dice?

> We met once when
> a surge slid us past one
> another. Hidden
> pools propel tongues
> of ice to speak to each
> rapidly as if words
> would melt from the heat
> of earth's inner cavities.
> These polished slopes, ridges
> or caps, none are accidental.

Acknowledgments

"Attachment" from *The Untidy Season*: An Anthology of Nebraska Women Poets. The Backwaters Press. Fall 2013.

"Bearded Swimmer" *Coe Review*. Fall 2009.

"Bearded Swimmer" *Rabbit Ears: TV Poems*. Poets Wear Prada. Spring 2014.

"Butte" *Fine Lines*. Summer 2010.

"Commiserating with Another Parent" *I-70 Review*. Winter 2012.

"Farm" *The Storm is Coming Anthology*. Sleeping Cat Books. March 2012.

"Glacier" *Midwest Quarterly*. Summer 2011.

"Matthew 13:33" *Sugar House Review*. Fall 2009.

"On Her Second Birthday" *Filling the Empty Room Anthology*. Morpo Press. February 2010.

"River" from *The Untidy Season*: An Anthology of Nebraska Women Poets. The Backwaters Press. Fall 2013.

"Steppe" *The Blue Bear Review*. December 2012.

"Tabula Rasa" from *The Untidy Season*: An Anthology of Nebraska Women Poets. The Backwaters Press. Fall 2013.

"To the Father of My Children" *Temenos*. Fall 2008.

"The winter moth orbits the light" *The Blue Bear Review*. December 2012.

Author Bio

Cat Dixon teaches creative writing at the University of Nebraska, Omaha, and she teaches composition at Metro Community College. She is board secretary for The Backwaters Press, and has volunteered with the press for eight years. Her work has appeared in numerous literary magazines and anthologies. *Too Heavy To Carry* is her first full length poetry collection. She is now at work on a collection of prayers and spiritual poems. She lives in Omaha with her children, Pierce and Leven, and her husband, Sky. To find out more, visit her website: www.catdix.com.

CPSIA information can be obtained at www.ICGtesting.com
Printed in the USA
LVOW08s0318210214

374641LV00005B/6/P